CHARTER,

BY-LAWS

AND

LIBRARY RULES

OF THE

OF PHILADELPHIA.

PHILADELPHIA:
KING & BAIRD, PRINTERS, 607 SANSOM STREET.
1870.

BOARD OF DIRECTORS

OF THE

MERCANTILE LIBRARY COMPANY

1870.

PRESIDENT.

T. MORRIS PEROT.

VICE PRESIDENT.

OLIVER H. WILSON.

RECORDING SECRETARY.

JOHN LARDNER.

CORRESPONDING SECRETARY.

JAMES G. BARNWELL.

TREASURER.

JOHN H. WATT.

DIRECTORS.

Joseph C. Grubb,
Richard Wood,
T Morris Perot,
Oliver H. Wilson,
Albert S. Letchworth,
John H. Watt,
S. E. Harlan,
Chas. M. Taylor,
Wm. A. Rolin,
James G. Barnwell,
John Lardner,
E. K. Stevenson,
Asa I. Fish,
Edward Taylor,
John S. Weimer,
Wm. D. Gemmill,
Oliver Evans,
Edward Bains.

LIBRARIAN.

JOHN EDMANDS.

CHARTER

OF THE

Mercantile Library Company of Philadelphia.

SECTION 1. Be it enacted by the Senate and House of Representatives of the Commonwealth of Pennsylvania, in General Assembly met, and it is hereby enacted by the authority of the same, That the Mercantile Library Company of Philadelphia is hereby enacted into a body politic and corporate, in deed, and in law, by the name, style and title of the "Mercantile Library Company of Philadelphia," and by the same name to have perpetual succession, be capable of suing and being sued, to have a common seal, and the same to alter and renew at pleasure, and shall be able and capable in law and equity to take and hold for the use of said Company, any real estate, goods, chattels, and sum or sums of money, by gift, grant, bargain, sale, will, devise or bequest, or otherwise, from any person or persons whomsoever, capable of making the same; and the same to grant, bargain, sell, and a good conveyance make for the use of the said Library, and generally to do all and singular the matters and things which may be lawful and necessary for them to do for the well being, and due management of the affairs thereof.

Sec. 2. That this corporation shall consist of all such persons as are now members, or shall be hereafter admitted as such, agreeably to the by-laws of said Company.

Sec. 3. The affairs of said Company shall be conducted by a Board of eighteen Directors, chosen by the stockholders. Seven members of this Board of Directors shall form a quorum for the transaction of business. At their first meeting after election, or as soon thereafter as possible, the Directors shall choose from their own number, a President, a Vice-President, a Recording Secretary, a Corresponding Secretary, and a Treasurer, who shall be the officers of the Company, and shall serve for one year, and until their successors shall have been duly elected.

The officers and Directors constituting the Board of Management when this amendment to the charter shall have been granted, shall, as soon as possible thereafter, elect one additional Director. They shall divide themselves into three equal classes: the first class shall hold office until the next annual election; the second class until the second annual election, and the third class until the third annual election thereafter. And at each annual election after the granting of this amendment, there shall be elected six Directors, to serve for three years, and until their successors shall enter upon their duties.

The annual election shall be held on the third Tuesday in February of every year. Each share of stock shall be entitled to one vote, to be voted by the owner in person. No person shall be eligible as a Director who is not a stockholder, of at least twenty-one years of age, and who shall not have been nominated for that position at the stated annual meeting next preceding the election; and votes which may be polled for any person not so nominated, shall not be counted. The Board of Directors shall have power to fill vacancies occurring in their own body.

SEC. 4. That the funds of this Company shall be raised by the sale of stock and of perpetual and life memberships, and also by annual dues from stockholders and payments by subscribers, and other lawful means, and shall be appropriated by the Board of Directors, in such manner as may appear to them most conducive to the interests of the Company.

SEC. 5. The Board of Directors shall have full power to make and alter such rules and by-laws as they may deem necessary for the well-being and due management of the affairs of the Company: Provided, such by-laws are not repugnant to nor inconsistent with this charter, or with the constitution and laws of this State, or of the United States.

SEC. 6. That a general meeting of the stockholders of the Company shall be held annually on the third Tuesday of January, in each year, at which the Board of Management shall produce a statement of the affairs of the institution for the preceding year, and such other business may be transacted as shall relate to the general interests of the Company.

BY-LAWS

OF THE

Mercantile Library Company of Philadelphia.

Stockholders and Subscribers.

1. Any person not under fifteen years of age, if approved by the Board of Directors, may become a stockholder of the Library Company in the following manner: by the payment of ten dollars for a share of common stock, by the payment of forty dollars for a share of life stock, or by the payment of one hundred dollars for a share of perpetual stock; and every stockholder shall be furnished with a certificate for each share of stock owned by him, bearing the seal of the Company and signed by the President and the Treasurer.

2. Common stock shall be subject to an annual tax of four dollars upon each share, which shall be due and payable at the Library upon the first of January in each year. If the tax is not paid prior to July first, a fine of twenty-five cents; if not paid prior to October first, a fine of fifty cents; or if not paid prior to January first of the succeeding year, a fine of seventy-five cents shall be imposed.

3. Life stock shall be free from any annual tax, and may, at the will of the holder, during his life, be converted into four shares of common stock, which shall be subject to

annual taxes as stated in Section 2; otherwise, it shall not be transferrable, and will expire at the death of the holder

4. Perpetual stock shall be free from any annual tax; shall be transferrable, and may, at the will of the holder, be converted into ten shares of common stock, which shall be subject to annual taxes as stated in Section 2.

5. Transfers of stock shall be made on the surrender of the original certificate, and the payment of all taxes and fines that may have accrued thereon, (and the necessary United States Internal Revenue Stamps); and all issues and transfers of stock shall be subject to the approval of the Board of Directors.

6. No person purchasing a share of stock (except directly from the Company) shall be admitted to the privileges thereof, until he shall have taken the necessary steps to have the share transferred; and no person shall be permitted to exercise any rights or privileges of membership until he has signed an obligation to conform to and abide by all the By-Laws, Rules and Regulations which have been or may be lawfully enacted by the Board of Directors.

7. Shares of stock upon which annual taxes or fines have been outstanding for two years shall be liable to forfeiture, but the forfeiture thereof shall be no bar to the recovery by law or otherwise, of the arrearages which may be due thereon.

8. The Board of Directors may admit persons over twelve years of age to the use of the Library and Reading Rooms upon the payment of six dollars a year, or four dollars for six months, in advance; (and they may also authorize the Librarian to permit temporary residents to use the Library upon such terms as may be prescribed by the Board.)

Duties of Board of Directors and Officers.

9. The Directors shall meet on the Thursday next following the annual election for the purpose of organization and the transaction of other business.

10. They shall hold stated meetings at least once in each month, and special meetings whenever necessary.

11. The Directors shall have power to suspend or expel a stockholder or subscriber for violation of the Rules or By-Laws of the Company or for improper conduct.

12. No Director shall be allowed a salary or pecuniary compensation for his services.

13. Any Director who shall absent himself from the meetings of the Board for three consecutive months, without good cause and without leave being granted by the Board, shall be considered as having resigned, and the vacancy shall be filled by the Board.

14. The President shall call to order all meetings of the stockholders and shall preside thereat until a chairman shall have been chosen. He shall preside at all meetings of the Board, shall call special meetings of the Board whenever he shall deem it necessary, or upon the application of three Directors, and shall perform all the duties usually appertaining to the office.

15. The Vice-President in the absence of the President shall perform the duties of that officer.

16. The Recording Secretary shall keep an accurate record, in separate books, of all votes and transactions of the Company and of the Board of Directors. He shall file all written reports that are made, and give notice to all persons interested, of all votes of the Company and of the

Board. He shall give at least two weeks notice in two or more daily papers of all meetings of the Company. He shall be ex-officio one of the tellers of the election and shall read the report of the tellers at the next stated meeting of the Board. In the absence of the President and the Vice-President he shall call the meetings to order. He shall hand over to his successor in office, duly chosen, all books, papers and other property belonging to the Company in his possession.

17. The Corresponding Secretary shall conduct the correspondence of the Company, under the superintendence of the Board. He shall retain copies of all letters sent and file all that are received. He shall hand over to his successor in office, duly chosen, all books, papers and other property belonging to the Company in his possession.

18. The Treasurer shall, before entering on the duties of his office, give such security as the Board may think necessary for the faithful execution of the trust. He shall receive all taxes, rents, donations, bequests and other moneys due to the Company, and deposit the same with such bank or other institution of trust as may be designated by the Board, and he shall be the legal custodian of the title deeds and securities belonging to the Company, and of the account books and all papers and documents pertaining to his department. He shall pay no money from the treasury except on bills duly approved and orders drawn by the Board. He shall keep accurate accounts of all money transactions of the Company, and his books and papers shall at all times be subject to inspection by the Directors.

At each stated meeting of the Board he shall present an abstract of his accounts for the month, and a statement of all matters within the sphere of his duties requiring the action of the Board.

At the annual meeting of the Company he shall submit

to the stockholders a report embracing an abstract of his accounts for the year, and a full statement of the financial condition of the Company, and generally, he shall do and perform all the duties which usually appertain to the office.

He shall pay over to his successor in office, duly chosen and qualified, any balance of cash that may be in his hands and deliver up to him all books, papers and other property belonging to the Company in his possession.

Annual Meeting.

19. At the annual meeting of the Company the report of the Directors and of the Treasurer shall be read, nominations for Directors made and tellers appointed, who, with the Recording Secretary, shall conduct the annual election. A list of the nominations shall be printed and placed in the Library for distribution at least two weeks prior to the election.

Annual Election.

20. The annual election shall be held on the third Tuesday in February, between four and eight o'clock P. M., at which time six Directors shall be elected. Each share of stock shall entitle the owner thereof to one vote, the same to be polled in person ; but no stockholder shall be entitled to vote who is in arrears, for taxes or fines, that may have been incurred previous to the current year. Immediately after closing the polls the tellers and Recording Secretary shall proceed to count the votes, in the room where the election has been held, and announce the result. The Recording Secretary shall make a list of all the votes cast, to be signed by the tellers, which he shall produce at the next meeting of the Board. He shall also furnish a certificate of election, signed by the tellers, to each of those who may be elected.

If, after any election, it shall appear that the number of

persons required to be elected as Directors, has not been elected, by reason of two or more persons having received an equal number of votes, the Board shall, at their first meeting thereafter, proceed to fill the vacancy or vacancies, by election from the persons who received said equal number of votes.

Amendments to Charter.

21. Any proposed amendment or alteration to the charter, signed by twenty-five stockholders, and delivered to the President or Vice-President, not less than thirty days before the annual meeting, shall immediately upon its reception be posted upon the Bulletin Board.

If at the annual meeting a majority should appear to be in its favor, it shall be forthwith submitted to a stock vote of those present, at which time each share shall entitle its owner to one vote, and if carried, the Board of Directors shall send a copy of the proposed amendment to each stockholder, to be returned with his approval or disapproval within twenty days from the date upon which it is sent; whereupon, if a majority by this general stock vote shall have been in the affirmative, the Board shall apply to the proper authority to sanction the proposed amendment. In all such cases, each share of stock shall entitle its owner to one vote, and a record of such votes shall be kept in a book prepared for that purpose. Any stockholder having a right to be informed how his own vote has been recorded.

RULES FOR THE GOVERNMENT.

OF THE

LIBRARY AND READING ROOMS.

---

1. The Newspaper room shall be open from 7½ A. M. to 10 P. M., and the Library from 9 A. M. to 10 P. M., every day except Sunday; but on holidays no books will be received or delivered.

2. Stockholders and subscribers only are entitled to the use of the Library and reading rooms; except that they may send other persons for books, and that any stockholder may, by a writing revocable at his pleasure, designate a person qualified to hold stock, who shall be allowed to use the Library in his stead, and for whose observance of the rules of the Library he shall be responsible,—this writing to be filed with the Librarian.

3. If any stockholder or subscriber desires to protect his account from use by unauthorized persons, and possible loss thereby, he may obtain a ticket, which must be shown by himself, or any one else taking out books on his account.

4. No one shall be allowed to take out a book after the presentation of the bill for taxes, if they remain unpaid; nor if any fine or other charge against him shall be one month unpaid.

5. The Librarian may loan on each share or subscription, one work, or part of a work, not exceeding four volumes, and on any share of stock on which $3.00 annually is paid, in addition to the ordinary taxes, the same number of books as on two shares, provided the books are taken for the member's own use. Those who avail themselves of this privilege, will be required in all cases to present a ticket in order to get books. A volume of a periodical shall be considered a complete work.

6. Extra books may be loaned to stockholders and subscribers on payment of ten cents a week or part of a week for each volume.

7. Stamped orders for the delivery of books at residences, will be sold at the Library for five cents each. A member sending a properly stamped order, with a list of four books will be furnished with one, if in the Library, or purchasable in the city at a moderate price. Books already out must be returned by the messenger, or those delivered will be charged as extra books. The limits of delivery are:—from the Delaware River to the Schuylkill, and from Washington Avenue to Girard Avenue.

8. New books may be kept from the Library one week only, and not renewed; other books may be kept two weeks and renewed once only, provided no fine is due on them.

9. Any member who shall detain a book from the Library beyond the time prescribed in Rule 8, shall pay for each volume ten cents a week or a fraction of a week, for such detention.

10. If any member shall fail to return a book within two weeks after he shall have been requested to do so, the

Librarian is authorized to replace the volume detained and charge the cost thereof against the account of the delinquent.

11. Books purchased within six months of their publication, and such others as may be deemed of sufficient importance, shall be labelled as " new books," until transferred to their appropriate classes.

12. No book shall be reserved for any member.

13. Pamphlets and periodicals not numbered, and books set apart by the purchasing committee for use in the Library, and distinguished by a green label, shall not be taken from the Library without the consent of the book committee, and on conditions to be determined by them.

14. If any member shall take a book from the Library without having it charged to his account, his share, and all right to the use of the Library, shall thereby be liable to forfeiture.

15. Any member who shall lose or injure a book, shall replace the same, or pay an equivalent in money; and if the book be one of a set, he shall make the set complete and uniform, or pay for the whole of it, receiving the odd volumes as his property.

16. Cards may be obtained at the desk, by means of which a stockholder may introduce any non-resident by entering his name and residence upon the card, and becoming responsible for his deportment. This will entitle the holder to the use of the reading rooms for one month. But should any stockholder thus introduce a resident, his share shall be liable to forfeiture. These cards are not under any circumstances, transferrable.

17. Those not members, wishing to examine the rooms and Library, will be admitted for that purpose on registering their names and residences at the desk.

18. Conversation is allowed only in the conversation rooms.

19. Smoking in the rooms, spitting on the floor, placing feet on chairs or tables or against book-cases or windows, and defacing in any way the rooms or furniture are strictly prohibited.

20. The use of the reading rooms and chess tables, is restricted to shareholders and subscribers, and those to whom the use of a share has been regularly transferred.

21. The chess-men shall be placed upon the tables in the chess room for the use of the members.

22. The Librarian is vested by the Board of Directors with the government of the Library, and is required to observe and enforce each of the above rules in every particular, and without any exception.

www.ingramcontent.com/pod-product-compliance
Lightning Source LLC
LaVergne TN
LVHW020639110826
845149LV00004B/1282

9781418190460